Contents

Acknowledgements

All the images in this work come from the archive of PVEC, the Police Vehicle Enthusiasts' Club, which in 2016 is in its thirtieth year. The core of today's archive actually began in the mid-1960s and now incorporates individual archives donated by current and former officers and members – photographers and collectors united by a passion to record and understand a fascinating story. It's a story in which innovation comes and then is gone on what can be almost a daily basis.

Important collections include donations from the family of the late Eric McIntosh (EM), from Bob Chambers (BC), Paul Cook, John Oliver (JO) and Brian Homans (BH). Additional tribute must be paid to the two last named, without whom PVEC, and therefore the archive and the book, would not exist. Enormous thanks are also due, both for taking on major club responsibilities over time as well as for their prowess as photographers, to (alphabetically) Paul Billett, Alfons Blümmel, Jim Burns, Matt Holmes (MH), Alan Matthews (AM), Chris Pullen, Ian Stephenson and Chris Taylor (CT).

Other members have been both active and generous in their exchange of information and material, and they deserve recognition. Because of the way in which images have historically been shared, it is possible that the work of some may appear here uncredited, in which case apologies are due. Colin Chipperfield (CC), Simon Dixon, Gordon Feaver, John Parks and Richard Sweetman (RS) must be thanked for their knowledge and support, while the list of notable photographers must include Steven Adcock, Wilf Bainbridge, Andy Bardsley, Neil Barker, Dave Boulter MBE, Neil Cameron, David Devaynes, Neil Donaldson (ND), Colin Dunford (CD), Ian Farmer, Andrew Fenton, John Godwin, Steve Greenaway, Andrew Hunton, Colin Jackson, Iain Kitchen, Ian Marlow, Alex McKenzie, Bob Mileham, Paul Miller, Geoff Newbury, Steve Pearson, Ken Reid (Fire Fotos – FF), Geraint Roberts (GR), Paul Stubbings, Bob Storrar, Norman Tarling (NT), Roger Tennyson, Steve Vickers, James Waddington, Alex Watson, Paul Yarrington and Paul Young. Equally, apologies to anyone deserving of inclusion but missed out.

The letter codes given in brackets above identify images originating from individuals, while the addition of a letter C to codes denotes items from individuals' collections. In a small minority of cases, it has not been possible either to identify or to contact possible copyright holders, for which again apologies are offered.

Special thanks goes to PM Photography for permission to use images from their extensive commercially available transport lists and supplying scans.

I pay tribute to the handful of other writers who have, against the odds, led the way in having published the small number of earlier books dealing with aspects of British police transport, especially Peter Hall and Andrea Green. Recommended further reading appears in the appendix.

About the Author

Paddy Carpenter has had a long career as a writer and filmmaker, travelling extensively and working with many well-known names.

An early fascination with transport of all kinds was supplemented in schooldays by an interest in the history of the British police. The resulting combined study of police vehicles has been followed ever since and he has written extensively on the subject for both specialist publications and motoring magazines since the mid-90s.

A pilot for thirty years, he commentates on air racing for the Royal Aero Club. His understanding of aviation, the film industry and police matters led to the writing of his first novel *UNSAFE – The Script of One-Zero-Three*, in which the real evidence of the Lockerbie airliner bombing is reinvestigated, leading to startling conclusions.

Introduction

A Surprisingly Neglected Subject

Transport in all its forms has almost endless appeal, with every variety of mode and sub-group attracting both general interest and the attention of specialists. In road transport, every category, each make and even individual models have their adherents, often with clubs and publications specifically devoted to them; there can be books on dustcarts and brewers' drays. It's surprising, then, that until recent times British police transport has been so little recorded and studied. After all, police vehicles, with their bold liveries and added equipment, can look extremely appealing and the things they do are undeniably exciting.

Because of the fast turnover of vehicles, police fleets are constantly renewing – indeed, police transport is without doubt the fastest-changing aspect within the streetscape and its appearance will also vary a great deal according to locality. Even today there are forty-three territorial police forces in England and Wales and, until recent years, each had a totally independent policy on vehicle procurement – and on how they equipped and presented their fleets. Before 1974, there were more forces. In 1962, for example, the corresponding number was 125. Clearly the subject is a much larger one than might be realised and only an impression can be offered in one medium-sized book.

Several decisions have needed to be taken. Firstly, to focus, for the present offering, on patrol and response vehicles – the cars and vans filling those two functions, leaving for later motorcycles and other vehicles of a specialised nature, many fulfilling equally dramatic roles. Secondly, space dictates that the vehicles of Scottish forces and those of Northern Ireland, the Channel Islands, the Isle of Man and non-territorial forces such as the British Transport Police must also be held over for a later release.

Significantly, this work, which is the first to have the advantage of bringing the story to life in full colour, will use that ability to concentrate on what we will call the Golden Age, a period of some forty years during which a profusion of colour and individual liveries took over from the previous standard black and very dark blue.

As with the paint schemes of the traditional bus companies, the appearance of police vehicles in those years added to that essential feeling of local identity and provided variety

This 1954 Riley Pathfinder typifies the image that the British police car projected from the late 1930s to the mid-1960s – a large, shiny, black, powerful saloon. In fact the Pathfinder, like its RM predecessors, was a four-cylinder. Six-cylinder engines, as in the similar-looking Wolseley 6/90, were more common, but the Riley name held promise of sporty performance, and so kept some loyal customers, including the West Sussex Constabulary. (EMB)

and added interest to every long journey. Now that diversity has followed many of those other transport liveries into history, with the ungainly blue-and-yellow blocks of the Battenburg livery being foisted on the police by the Home Office.

Fortunately, before this finally happened, the neglected subject had attracted some enthusiasts, who were able to record at least some of the Golden Age in photographs. Also, many individual police officers were keeping informal collections of the transport they used at work. Such items are now increasingly coming to light. This is all fortunate as many police forces neglected to record their transport heritage and, when they did, many items were later lost or thrown in skips when forces amalgamated or when storage space was reassigned. What has been saved is minuscule in comparison to the profusion of material covering railways, buses, trams or cars, but the fact that even this amount survives is a credit to a relatively small and dogged band of photographers and researchers, many of whose names appear in the acknowledgements and the picture credits.

At the time of writing, the archive of the Police Vehicle Enthusiasts' Club contains something in the region of 50,000 images, an impressive figure but a drop in the ocean when that long list of past forces and the astonishing variety and numbers of their vehicles are given a moment's consideration. The gaps in our knowledge and coverage can be vast. That said, with so much material available, the selection of the best pictures to tell the story has been something of a marathon task. It has, however, been a highly enjoyable one and I hope that readers find the result equally so.

A Freight Rover Sherpa van of the Cumbria Constabulary wears a dark blue livery that was traditional to commercial types in most British police forces until the 1960s. Many, including London's Met, wore a shade of navy that was close to black. Cumbria was one force that continued with blue vans when its cars moved to white. Neighbouring Lancashire also kept blue in various shades for some of its vans. (JO)

How things would change. In pursuit of safety, police vehicles brought new colour to British roads and a by-product was exciting individuality, adding interest to travel by helping to differentiate one place from another. Warwickshire and Gloucestershire share a border, yet the traffic cars that would be encountered on its respective sides very successfully announced themselves, in strikingly different ways. Warwickshire Volvo 850 T5 and Gloucestershire Vauxhall Cavalier V6. (Both PC)

1

How Today's Police Forces Came About

Rowing Boats and Riding Boots

The average British citizen, if asked, is likely to come up with a handful of facts about the origins of our police service. Mostly, they won't be correct. A widespread belief is that the first proper force in the British Isles was London's Metropolitan Police. It wasn't. Several forces in Scottish burghs beat the Met's 1829 date. Glasgow, for example, had a police force in 1800; Dublin, which was British until 1922, had one as early as 1786. The square mile of the City of London had a uniformed day police in 1784. The Marine Police began protecting trade on London's river and wharves in 1798 and, although privately sponsored, it was the first force formed by an Act of Parliament.

Some will give the Bow Street Runners, founded in 1748, as the first police. Indeed, their actual name was the Bow Street Police, 'runners' being an unofficial popular title they eventually attracted. In reality, the runners were plain-clothes investigators, responsible for pursuing offenders once crime had been committed. Their presence and their successes were a deterrent, true, but they did not prevent crime by patrolling, which the later forces

By the date of this picture, 1864, the 1798 Marine Police Force had become the Thames Division of the Metropolitan Police. The means of patrol remained the same – rowing galleys, with either a sergeant and two oarsmen or an inspector with three – until the welcome arrival of motorboats in the 1920s.

did. What we regard as 'modern policing' began patchily in the late eighteenth century and spread to the entire nation during the mid-years of the nineteenth; it combined the two essential approaches to policing, preventive and reactive, which are most readily seen in the police's most visible activities, patrol and response.

The Bow Street magistrate Sir John Fielding (who had taken over on the death of his more famous brother, Henry, the novelist) moved into preventive policing with his introduction of the Bow Street Horse Patrol to combat highwaymen and footpads, who preyed on the main roads leading out of London. What followed has a very modern resonance. The incentive was so successful in deterring crime that highway robbery around London all but ceased. Actually, the perpetrators had relocated. Noting what appeared to be a major success, after eighteen months the government withdrew its funding as no longer necessary – an eighteenth-century cutback. The patrol was withdrawn; the shouts of 'stand and deliver' recommenced.

When the lessons of history are not learned, history repeats itself. In 2016, preventive policing in the streets and on the roads is largely a thing of the past. The results of that, which were easily predictable, are now becoming plain for all to see.

Who Needs Police?

Modern, adequate policing was slow in coming to Britain, despite a pressing need in London especially, where the crowding together of one in ten of Britain's inhabitants had sent crime levels soaring beyond any quantifying or control. It's true that some of the reluctance to introduce police was due to simple dislike of change, in addition to obstruction by vested interests. However, there was also widespread genuine fear of a force under the control of the government, which would hold powers that could be misused for factional advantage, just as had happened in France with horrific results. Parliament continually voted down any proposals, notably one for the whole of London from the Prime Minister, William Pitt, in 1785.

Progress came by small degrees; in 1792 six paid officers were attached to each of seven magistrates' offices across the capital. After five years, Bow Street led the way once more by instituting night patrols for Westminster and the principal highways. Armed but without uniform, the thirteen groups of four or five successfully reduced crime between dusk and midnight.

The Home Office had been set up in 1782 with the Home Secretary responsible for law and order. Noting the successes of the Runners, the Bow Street Foot or Night Patrol and the Marine Police, he reintroduced the Bow Street Horse Patrol in 1805. This force was uniformed and, with one item being a scarlet waistcoat, its officers became known as 'Robin Redbreasts'. This is usually claimed as the first uniformed force in the nation, but the City of London Day Police, or indeed others, will have taken that distinction.

In 1822, Robert Peel, Secretary for Ireland, introduced what was called the 'constabulary force' in that country. This forerunner of the Irish, later Royal Irish, Constabulary was essentially a paramilitary force of a type that the British parliament would not sanction for the mainland, but which could be imposed on a subservient Ireland.

The highly military nature of the constabulary police in Ireland may be gleaned from this contemporary engraving.

Thus we can see that the first modes of transport used by British police officers were horses and rowing boats. Additionally, for many years policemen walked – and clearly sometimes ran.

In 1828 that same Robert Peel became Home Secretary for the second time. His attempts to bring effective policing to the capital, let alone the countryside, met with the usual opposition, but he eventually won narrow approval to form the Metropolitan Police in 1829. When the positive results were seen, the government legislated to require other cities and boroughs to form police forces from 1835, with approval for counties to do so coming four years later. Take-up there was generally slow; an act obliging the institution countrywide had to follow, but it didn't come until 1856.

Forces in Play

The tardiness indicates the strength of opposition, which, if anything, increased in the early years. The new police faced hostility from all sides. Obviously, the criminal classes found their livelihood affected and incited all the opposition they could. At the opposite end of the social scale, the gentry were used to dispensing justice in the shires, which they largely interpreted as ensuring the status quo and safeguarding their own property. They regarded parish constables as minions serving that end, and deplored the idea that anyone from the lower orders could have any authority extending to their own adherence to the law. In any case, the countryside, they argued, was relatively peaceful, with a population under control – although there, too, things were about to change. In their view, there was no need for police and they certainly wanted nothing to do with paying for them.

The emerging rich in the towns, where there was more crime, felt the same way about contributing financially to its control and some of them too did not want their own activities put under independent scrutiny. In the middle, the law-abiding were squeezed, exploited by the rich and also robbed by people below them in the class structure. They wanted crime tackled but were hardly in a sound position to fund the task.

The debates on the introduction of police set the pattern of policing, which has in many respects existed ever since. To assuage the fears of a centralised and government-controlled force, British policing would be local, and not national: officers' allegiance would be to the Crown. Only in the case of the Metropolitan Police would the chief officer, the commissioner, be responsible to the Home Secretary. In the cities and boroughs, chief or head constables would report to 'watch committees' set up for the purpose in the 1835 act; these were sub-committees of the full town or city corporation.

In country areas, county councils did not yet exist, and so the justices in quarter sessions were initially given authority to establish paid police. As has been noted, widespread failure to do so caused the government to compel action in 1856. In 1888, other legislation instituted county councils throughout England. Police responsibility was handed to new standing joint committees, which consisted half of county councillors and half of justices of the peace.

Parliament's strong insistence that the new police should be free of direction by politicians meant that control of a force and its enforcement of the law was entirely vested in its chief constable. Once appointed, these figures exercised a remarkable degree of autonomy and independence. In theory, despite holding the pursestrings, no government or local council could direct a chief officer as to any course of action. This led to many remarkable disagreements over the years, but the principle was fundamental. It is one that

A modern chief constable. Paul West QPM MA headed the West Mercia Constabulary from 2003 to 2011. Supportive of the conservation of police transport history, he is pictured at the handover of a retiring Vauxhall Astra for PVEC preservation. *Left to right:* Alan Matthews, Ex-WMC – PVEC Vehicles Officer; Alan Harris WMC Fleet Manager; CC Paul West; the author.

Independence, coupled with local pride, led to an era of glorious expression of individual force identity, which was reflected in vehicle liveries and no better illustrated than by one of the Kent Constabulary's experiments. Note the enthusiasm with which the county and force name is blazoned on the side. That was used fleet wide. Not only were Kent's local designs infinitely more stylish and attractive than the national livery that would follow but they also reflected better science and were safer. (PC)

is now increasingly and subtly eroded by Westminster and Whitehall, to the extent that the police can now appear to be an agency of the government in a way that would have horrified the eighteenth- and nineteenth-century members of parliament, who anguished endlessly over just that prospect.

A Pattern Evolves … and Changes Begin

What emerged in terms of geography was that England, Wales and Scotland were policed by county or, in some cases, subdivisions of counties. Sussex and Suffolk had county councils and separate police forces for their east and west halves, while Yorkshire had forces for its three ridings – north, east and west. Dotted across county maps were city and borough forces – pockets of individual jurisdiction (there was no overlap, as seen in the US) where different practices, policies and uniforms prevailed. Needless to say, patterns and choices relating to transport were also diverse, giving a variety that can be endlessly fascinating, when and if it can be discovered.

In 1857 there were 239 individual police forces in England and Wales, with eighty-nine in Scotland. Unsurprisingly, the process of consolidation and amalgamation began almost immediately, with the realisation that multiple, convoluted boundaries and very small forces could be a great impediment to efficiency. However, civic pride proved strong and a determination within towns and cities to maintain their own forces meant that many survived even into the 1970s. The City of London force exists separately to this day. In 1930, when forces began using mechanised transport in earnest, there remained still some 183 forces south of the border, with forty-nine in Scotland.

There are other popular misconceptions about the constabulary, many affecting transport. The bobby's bicycle is an icon of the British police, and people assume its use was automatic from the very early days. Not only was this not possible, due to the safety bicycle not coming into general use until the last years of the nineteenth century, but, in many cases, the use of cycles for patrol was expressly forbidden.

Cycles eventually became the norm for suburban and rural beats, and for sergeants doing their rounds. Some forces actually formed cycle sections as the earliest example of fast response, but often officers provided their own bikes and received an allowance. A Leicester City officer is seen patrolling a new housing estate in the 1950s or 60s.

This represents a consistent feature of the story of the British police: namely the institution's conservatism, and resistance to change in its way of working, plus a notable reluctance to accept valuable new inventions and ideas. A supreme example, with a clear bearing on the police duty to respond to events, is a report from a senior officer, who was evaluating a new development in communications. He wrote that to have members of the public able to make contact with police via the public telephone network 'would upset the whole running of a police station'.

It's true that some forces were much more reactive and prepared to experiment and innovate, principally due to being led by energetic and farsighted chief constables. Those forces would lead the way in the development of advances such as police boxes, two-way radio, traffic policing and panda cars. People think of London's Met as the world's foremost force, but it was often some way behind. To be fair, this was probably due to its size and the consequent cost implications of even the smallest change, coupled with its direct and undoubtedly restrictive relationship with the Home Office.

From 1856, that body had begun to influence the other police forces in the country. The Inspectorate of Constabulary was formed to assure central government that forces were being run properly and efficiently. To receive the government's contribution to its running costs, each one had to pass an annual visit and assessment. If it failed, it had to improve quickly or risk losing its grant. Continuing inefficiency could spell amalgamation. It is impossible on the evidence over the years not to see the Home Office as having the ambition to gain ever more control over police; to erode the statutory independence of chief constables; to suppress force individuality and to amalgamate forces progressively in the direction of one national police force.

If there is any doubt about that, note the success of the counterpart Scotland Office, which with the coming of the Scottish government has achieved exactly that – the total reverse of the theory and practice of policing carefully framed for our two nations nearly 190 years ago.

For those interested in transport, the end of individual Scottish forces means one vehicle-purchasing policy and one livery. There is not a great deal more to be enthused over south of the border, now that one livery reigns supreme, although there are minor variations to excite at least some interest. In comparison with the Golden Age, it has to be admitted that there is far less visual excitement. But things will change again, as they always have.

Are there any other popular police transport misconceptions to put right? Here is just one more for now, but others will come to light as the story unfolds. Younger readers, if they have heard of the Flying Squad, might well, from their perspective of today, think it involves helicopters. Older readers might, more correctly, believe that it has long involved the use of fast and powerful cars. Both parties will be surprised to hear that for their first transport, when inaugurated just after the First World War, the elite detective unit relied on a hired, horse-drawn covered wagon belonging to a railway company. These were followed by rather unwieldy motorised counterparts – lorries acquired secondhand after service with the Royal Flying Corps. These were the first instance of motorised patrol being undertaken by the British police, albeit covertly.

With luck, other myths will be punctured in the course of the pages that follow. Previous books on the subject have not been error-free – indeed, one officially sponsored publication had dozens of them. I hope there are many fewer here, but please advise us to correct any you may find. I was amused to read in a recent release that the oldest form of police car is the panda. For the truth on that matter and a host of others, read on. Welcome to the enthralling story of police patrol and response vehicles.

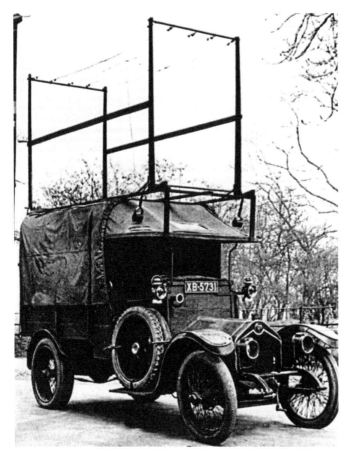

The Flying Squad's ex-RFC and RAF Crossley tenders achieved fame by being involved in early radio telegraphy experiments. Aerials would need to become less obvious before these vehicles could resume their habitual undercover role.

2

The Story

The Hundred Years' Walk

To understand the story of police transport, it's necessary to glance briefly at the contemporary wider transport picture. The spread of modern policing through Britain coincided with the railway-building era. On the roads, the horse remained in charge, as it did on the canal network. On the waterways, horse-drawn barges conveyed the bulk raw materials and distributed the products of the industrial revolution in a way that the rutted turnpike roads could never have handled. Those were the preserve of the local carter, the riding horses and personal carriages of the well-to-do, and the post-coaches for the minority who could afford to use them.

Before the railways, ordinary people travelled very little, if at all. Steam trains changed that and brought an unexpected consequence – a threat to that previously mentioned social stability in rural areas. In addition to this, the continuing industrialisation blurred distinctions between town and countryside where there was mining, quarrying or manufacture. Unrest caused by agricultural mechanisation completed the picture. It became clear that professional police were needed out in the counties as well as within the urban areas.

Many of the new forces took Peel's Metropolitan force as a pattern and, indeed, many of the early London constables were poached to train or even lead them. That model involved a parade for briefing at the start of a shift and marching out of the station, the party dividing until reaching individual allocated beats.

A beat was a patrol of a set of streets following a closely defined route and timetable. The timing involved prompt attendance at fixed locations. When the rank structure became refined, these would become known as conference points, where a sergeant or inspector could meet the constable to pass information, receive reports or simply check that all was 'in order'. This became an underlying and largely unchanged feature of British policing for more than 130 years, only ending with the coming of viable personal radio.

Another type of duty involved 'fixed points', which in London in the 1860s began to include 'point duty', the control of vehicles at busy junctions, often for the benefit of

As late as the 1960s constables could be seen marching out of stations to their allotted beats. Here a relief leaves the imposing headquarters of the Leicester City Police after parade.

pedestrians. This was the first public sign of police being routinely concerned with road traffic, an aspect of their work that would grow massively.

At least one county force, that of Gloucestershire, used a different operational method based on the model of the Irish Constabulary, where the first chief officer had previously served. It involved police living in barracks and patrolling in groups. Hostility to the police was widespread, but some parts of the British Isles remained especially lawless and potentially dangerous both for strangers and for anyone in authority.

Both the Marine Police and the Bow Street Horse Patrol were eventually incorporated into the Metropolitan Police, but it can be seen that, overwhelmingly, law and order was maintained on foot. When transport came into use, it was for the most senior only. A horse would have been the most suitable means for a chief constable to visit stations, especially in large areas. Horse-drawn two and four-wheelers – traps, hansoms and dog carts – might be used by others, and these seem to be the mode most usually adopted by superintendents and inspectors making their rounds, or high-ranking detectives attending cases. The lower orders would walk, or use public transport when appropriate. Prisoners were marched to the station, to court and, if guilty, to prison, often for many miles. Somewhat strangely, transport for these types of transfer represented one of the earliest steps towards the full range of vehicles that we now take for granted.

It will come as a surprise to many to learn that, in these early days, the police in many places were responsible both for fire-fighting and an emergency ambulance service. This saw the police using both simple, wheeled stretchers and handcart-type fire appliances, as well as horse-drawn steam fire pumps, escapes and proper ambulances.

All these categories of vehicle would become motorised but, as we have seen, the only one so far to fall into the categories of patrol or response is the use of vehicles by the Flying Squad. Formed by the Met in response to a surge in crime following the First World War, the squad (famously 'The Sweeney' in Cockney rhyming slang) was a plain-clothes unit of detectives, charged with busting the gangs through patrol, by observation – 'keeping obbo' – and by intervention and pursuit. The Manchester City Police and others followed London's lead in forming their own flying squads.

Used for medical emergencies, drunks and violent prisoners alike, the Bischoffsheim Hand Ambulance was charitably provided, but used by the police from 1860 until 1938. This one is seen at Uxbridge police station in 1934 with a new Fordson station van behind the group.

The Met Flying Squad would go on to use Lea Francis, Invicta, Bentley and Railton motor cars, while Manchester was using this Alvis Silver Eagle in the early 1930s. The car was also used for uniformed patrol – something of a giveaway.

A sobering fact in reference to the Met is that, through the 1920s, apart from the roving undercover patrols of the Flying Squad, there were cars to transport senior officers, motorcycles to convey messages, large vans to move prisoners, and smaller ones to carry paperwork; yet mechanised transport was not thought necessary for patrol and response, which continued on foot. Much the same was found outside London. This was about to change.

An Act Brings Action

The 1930 Road Traffic Act was the government's response to the growing tide of motor-car use and the horrific rise in road casualties that came with it. The act required all police forces to institute motor patrols to improve driving behaviour, firstly by example, secondly by giving advice, and thirdly through prosecution when necessary. The scale of grants paid to forces initially encouraged motorcycles, combinations (that is, motorcycles with

Rochdale Borough's first motor patrols typify the response of many forces to the requirements of the 1930 Act. Note that some of the sidecars are two-man. A motorcycle, three large men and substantial sidecar could not have been too speedy, which was perhaps just as well.

Combinations must have been particularly hair-raising at speed on Caernarvonshire's twisting mountain roads, and officers must have been delighted when, in 1934, they were replaced by Hillman Aero Minxes, seen here outside the Hillman factory. (JOC)

passenger sidecars) and three-wheel types rather than four-wheel tourers and saloons. However, when a number of accidents showed combinations especially to be unsuitable for high-speed police work, proper four-wheelers came into their own.

The motor patrols, whatever the government's intention, naturally became concerned with crime as well as road traffic. Whether through criminals themselves using vehicles, known offenders being spotted in the streets, or members of the public stopping police to report crime in progress, the mobile police could not help but become involved in matters other than motoring. However, just as for their colleagues on foot, there was one factor preventing them from being very much more effective in response to both crime and road-traffic incidents – and that was the lack of efficient communication and direction.

Once again London's Flying Squad had led the way by having radio hidden in its commercial types and the fast cars that superseded them. It was not, however, the convenient radio familiar for many years now. It was, instead, radio telegraphy, using Morse code and not speech; initially it was only one-way, transmitting from base to car but not vice-versa. Two-way came rapidly, but sets remained heavy and required a highly trained radio operator, straining to hear and decode a weak, variable signal while potentially on the move at speed in a swaying vehicle with rudimentary springs.

While experimentation continued to develop ever-better radio, an interim lower-tech advance in communications was spreading, although fairly slowly. This was the police-box system, which had appeared in Glasgow as early as 1891, but reached London only in late 1929. The idea was to place dedicated telephones at strategic places in an urban area. Fitted with a conspicuous flashing light to indicate that any officer seeing it should use it to contact the station, the installations ranged from a simple telephone pillar, to the box type (as made famous by *Doctor Who*), to what could with some forces be almost a miniature police station, with a rudimentary kitchen and even a holding cell.

Through the telephones in the boxes or pillars, messages could reach both beat men and motor patrol far more quickly than relying on conference points or scheduled return to stations. The boxes with shelter allowed the eating of refreshments, cutting out time

A PR photograph shows an early Metropolitan Police box. Later the signage would be changed to the familiar POLICE PUBLIC CALL BOX to highlight its availability to the public to call for assistance. The station van was a larger model of 1933 Fordson and interestingly had no offside door, the driver accessing it from the pavement side.

wasted off the beat walking to stations, and all offered the public a chance to contact the police for assistance or with information, usually by a separate telephone.

Part of the scheme in London involved a new class of vehicle, the station van, which would attend urgent calls from the boxes, sometimes bringing several officers, depending on circumstances. This then was part officer transport, part old-style Black Maria; it would carry first aid and sometimes items like a stretcher, a jack, a broom and some basic tools. Being kept ready at the station rather than patrolling, the station van can lay claim to being the first pure response vehicle.

As the 1930s progressed, technical improvements meant that mobile radio telephone – communication using speech instead of Morse code – had progressed. The go-ahead chief constable of Nottingham recognised that radio had great potential for the tactical direction of police vehicles, both to locations where incidents were happening, and during any subsequent chases. While his technical staff improved the hardware, he devised systems to cover all eventualities, systems that with updating remain in use in today's control rooms. He introduced to Britain the concept of the area wireless car. Unlike the Motor Patrol, with its concentration on motor traffic, the wireless car or area car, as it became variously known, would focus on crime.

A picture capturing the white heat of technology of yesteryear; a health and safety nightmare in today's terms. There was no room beside this Nottingham City police driver for a radio operator. He was it. The radio itself occupied the passenger seat. The officer is seen steering with his left hand and tapping out Morse code messages with his right. How he wrote down the letters he recognised from the incoming beeps in his headphones is not disclosed. Fortunately, technology progressed.

In larger forces, this would signal a separation of responsibility, which saw some elements of motor patrol move in the direction of a separate traffic division, generally at this time remaining non-radio. In smaller or less well-funded forces, when radio arrived, motor patrol fulfilled both traffic and crime functions.

Any advances were then put on hold for six years or more as Europe went to war yet again. The supply of new vehicles all but dried up, and transport of all types saw years of very hard use combined with under-maintenance. Many police officers served in the armed forces, leaving the police service reliant on retired reservists and on special constables, but it coped. Some amalgamations were ordered in the name of wartime efficiency and others followed just after the war. At the end of hostilities, the nation was all but bankrupt. With its infrastructure ravaged, it faced another post-war crime wave.

Post-War Blues

When car production resumed in 1945, the same models from the late 1930s rolled out of British car factories. Most of the production went for overseas orders, as 'export or die' was a slogan not too far removed from the truth. Police forces were given precedence in the long waiting lists and were able to start work on renewing their war-weary fleets. As the decade progressed, the first of the post-war designs began to come through, although most of the changes were superficial; engineering progress would follow later. Cars continued to remain in short supply, with the majority of those on British roads still pre-war in date.

The most common police patrol vehicle type at this time was that large saloon, typically with a six-cylinder engine. Such a specification provided sufficient power for a two-way radio. Radio sets were still bulky and weighty, and their batteries drew heavily on a car's charging system. Small cars couldn't cope; indeed, Wiltshire Constabulary recorded that the Rover P3 was not really up to the task of a wireless car and that its successor, the P4 Rover 75, was better. Large saloons offered reasonable performance, even with the drag arising from the heavy equipment on board, and they provided space for prisoners, which would

A Wiltshire Constabulary Rover 75 P4, deemed fit for wireless. Somewhat anticipating the age of colour, Wiltshire cars were green instead of black. Oddly, distant Cheshire also favoured green patrol cars and ran several generations of Rover P4s as well.

The interior of a 1950 City of London Wolseley 6-80 area wireless car shows much more user-friendly radio equipment, although there would still be heavy boxes in the boot. Speech has replaced Morse. The car's call-sign, OJ4, today spoken as 'Oscar Juliet Four', would then have been rendered 'Oboe Jig' or 'Oboe Johnny'. (RSC)

Apart from speed, which was useful for enforcement, open sports cars with uniformed figures in them had a PR and image function that some forces believed outweighed their basic impracticality. While Lancashire, with its large fleet, favoured them, principally MGs, numerous forces used small numbers, typified by the Southend-on-Sea Constabulary, which ran this single Triumph TR4 from 1962. (JOC)

be lacking in smaller vehicles. In this time of austerity, there were almost no British sports saloons being built, and so for sheer speed and pursuit ability, the choice was limited to out-and-out sports cars, suitable for working traffic non-radio, or something on two wheels.

Some forces, such as Lancashire Constabulary, had long favoured sports cars and continued to do so into the seventies; others would have nothing to do with them. Most forces, however, ran some motorcycles for traffic patrol. Perhaps even more than the cars, these were simply improved versions of pre-war models.

On four wheels it was the Wolseley marque that typified the age. Models such as the 6/80 of 1948 to 1954 and its successors, the 6/90, 6/99 and 6/110, almost always in gleaming black, achieved immortality. This was largely thanks to their small, illuminated bonnet badge light, which, when spotted at night in a rear mirror, sent shivers through many a motorist, whether speeding or not. Indeed, the car could easily belong to a local doctor or businessman instead of 'the law', but you just never knew until it was too late.

The exterior of the City of London 6/80 shows the usual Wolseley cues: curvaceous lines and the attractive radiator shell with the unique lit badge, topped with a flying W. For years the Met Police bought little else but Wolseleys – and many forces up and down the country followed suit. (RSC)

Of course, the move to saloons from open cars had meant a growth in the use of police signs too. When an open car had contained two figures with dark tunics and uniform caps, the message was fairly strong. With the crewmembers in a car's dark interior, their deterrent effect was diluted. Signs helped. Of course, there was usually a shiny bell to 'gong' a transgressing driver to a halt, but police signs with separately switched STOP panels gained growing acceptance. In those days, vehicles were stopped by overtaking them, so the STOP signs were rear-facing.

Wolseleys did not hold sway everywhere. Forces in areas where cars were built tended to favour a local manufacturer where they could. Local dealerships could exert a similar influence on some smaller forces. This meant that large Fords, Vauxhalls, Rovers, Jaguars and others predominated in some localities.

Despite an ongoing dribble of amalgamations, there were still 159 separate UK territorial police forces in 1961, so there was good scope for variety. Few forces dressed even identical cars in the same fashion as their neighbours, meaning that cars of the era can often be placed by the equipment they carried, in addition to the evidence of their registration plate.

White is the New Black

The glossy black aspect was set to change too. It had never been totally the case across the board. The City of Glasgow Police, for one, took some of its deliveries in a wide range of manufacturers' standard colours. Cheshire Constabulary's patrol cars were green, as were those of Somerset. Most police vans were not actually black, but very dark blue. Nevertheless, there were general conventions and they were about to be challenged by one of those innovative chief constables, the splendidly named Lt-Col Eric St Johnston (the name is pronounced 'Sinjenson'), heading the Lancashire force. In December 1958 his county was to see the opening of the first length of motorway in the British Isles. The Lancashire Constabulary was then the largest police force in the nation, after London's Met. It already had a reputation for forward thinking.

St Johnston's plan for the new challenge of policing motorways was to use for patrol a mix of estate cars to deal with incidents and sports cars for enforcement. For increased visibility, he had black vehicles resprayed white, a fairly rare colour for cars at the time. It is understood that the Home Office, always in favour of uniformity, disliked this incentive. The mandarins found the move that followed even less to their liking.

The Ford Zephyr Six Mk II with an estate conversion by Abbott of Farnham would become an integral component of several forces' approach to the business of policing the first UK motorways. This 1958 Lancashire example displayed its equipment in advance. Before the opening, this car would be resprayed white. The Golden Era was dawning.

Lancashire's motorway strategy in a single photograph. It is impossible today to appreciate just how much of a radical change these white cars represented. (CCC)

When car makers began to offer white as a regular option and the stand-out value of the colour was lost, Lancashire cars were decorated with large areas of DayGlo orange. Thanks to the autonomy of chief constables, Lancashire's innovations could not be suppressed and soon white traffic vehicles were seen countrywide, with reflective sidestripes following in turn. White eventually became the base colour for most police vehicles for more than fifty years.

As might be suspected, the Metropolitan Police was slow to follow the trend, not ordering white cars for traffic patrol until 1965. Black area cars remained the rule in the capital until the end of Jaguar S-Type production in 1968. The following Rover P6s and Triumph 2000 variants were not available in black, and there was nothing for it but to take large fleets in manufacturers' shades of blue, most notably Zircon Blue, a pleasing shade that gave an unaccustomed individuality to a large proportion of the London police fleet for several years.

The Mark ll Triumph 2000 had stunning lines, which could even cope with Lancashire Constabulary's application of DayGlo-orange paintwork. The model was very widely used, especially in its 2.5PI version, which crews liked but fleet managers and engineers didn't, due to reliability problems. Later research by the Transport & Road Research Laboratory would show that this livery approached perfection in safety terms. (JOC)

A Met Police Rover P6 3500 V8 wears the Zircon Blue paintwork, which enlivened the capital in the 1970s. This preserved example is seen next to an example of its Triumph contemporary, a 2.5PI, in a 'jam sandwich' livery with the black vinyl C-post and its small PI badge. Such cars shared the Met area car duties with the P6, also mainly in Zircon Blue, and they never carried a sidestripe, although some late traffic P6s in white did get the Met's first design. (JO)

Bears in Blue

By this time an even greater change was under way, and again it had its origin in Lancashire. The 'unit beat' scheme was devised to cover two challenges: firstly, that of maintaining an efficient service in a time of a chronic manpower shortage; secondly, how to police a troublesome overspill estate, created in Lancashire's territory to rehouse Liverpool residents displaced by slum clearance. The concept was only made possible by the development of viable personal radio, again a feature that Lancashire had pioneered. The scheme did away with the universal station parade at the start of each shift, for some officers at least. These 'home beat' officers lived in police houses and organised their patrols of their own area, booking on and off by radio. Backing up several beats was a new type of cheap and basic police vehicle. The eye-catching livery was American inspired, a simplified version of that used in Chicago, which city Chief Constable St Johnston had visited. A chance remark in the force workshop led to the name 'Panda Car'. Unit beat policing went nationwide after 1966 and, although the livery was not used everywhere, and was later simplified by most forces before eventually falling out of use, the name stuck – 'panda' became the name for any small, low-performance, basic police unit.

Everything changes. The Ford Anglia 105E, with its reverse-rake rear window, was a ground-breaker in itself. Its adoption as a police vehicle signalled the most significant shift since the coming of the first mechanised police transport. In this first production batch of Lancashire cars, note that the white roof stripe does not reach the windscreen. Later the stripe normally would.

London's first unit beat schemes also used Anglias as pandas, but the Morris Minor 1000 soon became more widespread and eventually iconic, despite several competing types. Already a twenty-year-old design in 1967, it somehow suited the role. This preserved example was used by the Bristol Constabulary. (PC)

Any number of models wore the panda livery. Equally, many pandas didn't. The officer's unique cap band tells us that Newcastle City Police Imps made do with a lettered panel and no stripe. The cars, however, *were* light blue. (JOC)

On cost grounds, the panda livery generally came to be simplified, as on this 1972/3 Austin 1100, operated and preserved by the Metropolitan Police. (PC)

The advent of panda cars was revolutionary in that it heralded a massive increase of small, marked patrol vehicles. These included vans, formerly mainly seen in rural areas, where they had sometimes been preferred to light motorcycles, which themselves had replaced pedal cycles. Panda vehicles stood out, as well as being numerous.

The evolving reliable, lightweight, wireless technology additionally meant that gone were the days when traffic and area cars needed to be large and powerful just to run a radio. Growing numbers of mid-size cars appeared in the area-car role, where load-carrying ability was less important than it was with motorway and divisional traffic units.

Another American-influenced livery trend had been seen on the cars of a scattering of forces in England and Scotland. They had adopted or experimented with a variety of bold black-and-white schemes for traffic units; Durham persisted with the attention-getting design for some while.

There is not space even to list the types used as pandas between 1966 and the early '80s, when the last deliveries of light-blue vehicles took place. Dark-blue and all-white 'pandas' would continue almost indefinitely. Here a Cheshire Austin Maestro van complies with the panda spirit in around 1986. (JOC)

On the area car front, Nottingham City Police had used Standard Triumph products since a batch of Vanguard Estate area cars in the 1950s. Tradition continued in 1963 with the use of the Ensign – a budget, four-cylinder version of the contemporary Vanguard – also in the use of the city coat of arms, showing particularly well on the force's first white patrol cars. Nottingham would, surprisingly, revert to black with its later delivery of Triumph 2000s. (CCC)

The resurgence of sports saloon production saw some take-up of the type for traffic cars, supplementing the more usual larger saloons. Northumberland, having found that MG Magnettes were suited to its rural road network, turned to the two-door and very stylish Sunbeam Rapier when the Farina Magnette III proved nowhere near as capable. (JOC)

Three views of English 'Black & Whites' prove that there was nothing standard about what was perceived as a 'typical' US cruiser livery. White door and boot panels are the only common factors in the West Riding of Yorkshire scheme on a Ford Zephyr IV and a Durham Constabulary version on an Austin A110 Mk II Westminster ... (CCC)(JOC)

... while Salford City Police had been there several years earlier with yet another arrangement – one incorporating the city coat of arms and bold force titling. Strangely, no black-and-white scheme trialled or adopted in the British Isles ever exactly reflected that of the California Highway Patrol, which had been featured on a popular television show here. The car is a Morris Oxford III. (MHC)

A further innovation was the carrying of force badges. Most had long applied a coat of arms or other identification to their commercial types, their Black Marias or station vans especially. Only one, the equally trailblazing Nottingham City Police, had added them to cars; indeed, they had done so since the 1930s. As far as is known, it had remained unique in the practice until 1958, when Glasgow City Police put bold lettering and the Scottish police badge on the front doors of a white Ford Consul. Now this practice would roll out across the British Isles.

Salford was very close in time to Glasgow in placing a badge on front-line car doors, and so it was a surprise to see go-ahead and adjacent Lancashire well beaten in that respect. The first door badges there date no earlier than 1965. This workshop yard view includes a wartime Chevrolet C15A Edbro recovery vehicle. (CCC)

Durham too seems to have pipped Lancashire by a few months. Badges on black cars were very rare and this style of badge, being not mounted on a Brunswick Star, was even more so. This Austin Westminster looks rather as if it should have belonged to Customs & Excise. (JOC)

Because they patrolled the 1965 extension of the M1 through the county, these Leicestershire & Rutland Constabulary Jaguar 3.8 Mk II saloons were high profile and the first badged cars of which many people became aware. The inset ad proves that Jaguar, in common with other makers like Ford, now understood that police sales could influence private buyers to the benefit of a company's trading figures.

With eye-catching liveries and the use of force badges spreading, there was one further development that was going to change forever the appearance of police vehicles. That was the availability of reflective and fluorescent tape and vinyl sheet. Using these, any unit could be marked up with flashes or panels to render them much more readily visible by day or night, with the DayGlo effect working during the day and the reflective taking over by night. The invention of the sidestripe is generally credited to George Terry, later knighted, chief constable of East Sussex.

Police workshops began to apply stripes or bands, generally thin ones at first, but they grew in width and complexity over time. Once an individual force had experimented and found a particular combination it liked, it tended to stick with it (happy pun) and the sidestripe became part of each force's identity. At first it was only the front-line traffic cars that received the treatment but, as time passed, the practice would widen to other types, as we shall see.

The Golden Age of British police vehicles could begin.

The first known picture of a proper sidestripe is a black and white image showing a pair of the East Sussex Constabulary's 1966 MGB GTs. Colour views of the force's ground-breaking red reflective/orange fluorescent/red reflective arrangement are rare. Here it is worn by a 1971/2 Mark II Triumph 2.5 PI. Sussex's five forces merged in January 1968 and, as seen, the stripe was adopted by the new Sussex Constabulary, though it was replicated by few others. (Dr Clifford Grey)

Oddly, it wasn't East Sussex's pioneering scheme that would become the nearest thing to a 'standard' as any contender achieved, but rather the blue/red or orange/blue stripe that entered the public consciousness under the somewhat incongruous name of 'Jam Sandwich'. It appears here on a Hertfordshire Hillman Hunter GT area car. The Hunter and its more basic Minx counterpart were used by most forces in some capacity. (JOC)

3

Patrol and Response Vehicles in England and Wales

Simply Red

Very few forces emulated the original East Sussex livery design. One that tried it for a while, but much later, was Wiltshire Constabulary. That force gained a name for trying an almost endless array of vehicles and numerous variations of livery, so much so that a book could be produced on Wiltshire alone. Brand-new and looking suitably smart is a BMW 528i, a late E28 model from 1986/7. (JOC)

The Leyland Daf Sherpa 200 station van with its large badge and POLICE graphic was a feature of Manchester and its Greater Manchester Police over a long period. The livery stripe is of an even simpler design than Sussex's, being a single band of DayGlo. (JO)

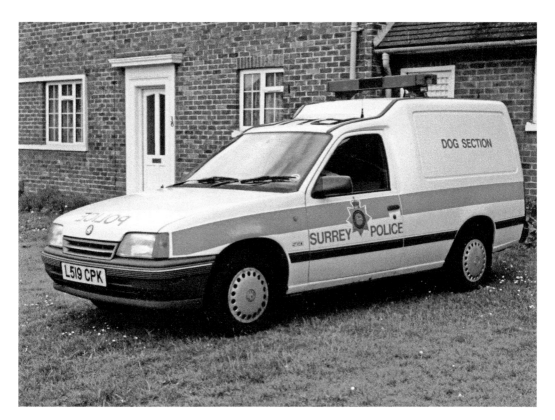

For a long period, Surrey Constabulary's choice of stripe was similar to Manchester's, but somewhat bolder. By the time of this Astramax 560 Dog Van, the force had sadly changed its name. That did lead though to some outstandingly clear force titling on doors. Rarely equalled anywhere, the excellent graphics were all-too-soon replaced by something not a tenth as good – a familiar recurrence throughout this story.

And Simply Orange. Some of West Mercia Constabulary's predecessors may have turned briefly to more conventional stripes, but the 1967 force first decorated the front doors of its traffic units in a shade actually known as Truck Yellow. A plain, matching stripe soon followed.

Carrying superstructure that brings a water-vessel to mind, there's no mistaking the very forthright and purposeful Senator I. The broadish version of the sandwich is complemented by the shield of the Leicestershire force's coat of arms, incorporating charges from Leicestershire, Rutland and the City of Leicester, the force's antecedents.

A thinner sandwich but more fine heraldry and classic force identification adorn this early Granada II, a Hertfordshire traffic car in private preservation. The coat of arms belongs to the county council, rather than the police force, but for years no one minded – and why should they? The Granada II was the market leader in its day. (BH)

More of the same: another Granada, a Mark III Fastback; a thin, high-set stripe; undoubtedly the most attractive coat of arms ever worn by a police vehicle, that of Nottinghamshire Constabulary; and even force identification, although not very visible, due to its position on the sidestripe. This style and positioning of titling was shared with Wiltshire Constabulary for many years. (BCC)

And again. This car stole the crown from Ford, for the Granada III was not widely liked, while the Senator II did the job for many. Both, however, faced increasing foreign competition, if 'foreign' had any real meaning, as both Granadas and Senators were built in Germany. This 1990 Thames Valley twenty-four-valve example exhibits the earlier version of the motorway livery with the force arms on the rear doors and the blue stripes omitted on the doors to allow larger POLICE graphics. (BCC)

... Jam Tomorrow

There was some home-grown competition still about. The Mk II Rover 800 series, when fitted with the Honda engine, was thought not bad by some. It certainly looked the part as a fastback or as a saloon. This Coventry-registered demonstrator wears the full Devon & Cornwall livery of the time. (CCC)

The last hurrah with the police for the Jaguar XJ6 was the PS, Police Special, version of the Mk V. By this time, due to price, size and probably image, it was bought by a very much reduced number of forces, of which Staffordshire was one. The force's green badge, with its Stafford knot emblem, is very distinctive. To accommodate it without interfering with the striping, a high stripe was employed, giving a perhaps more dated look than the superb lines deserved. (PC)

As with neighbour Hertfordshire, Bedfordshire Police 'borrowed' the county council arms for many years to very attractive effect; they even survive to bedeck this 97/8 Vauxhall Omega I. At that time, livery enhancements such as the orange on the C-posts showed that thought was being given to improving the conspicuity of cars attending incidents on high-speed roads. (CC)

Another 827i saloon, the property of Northumbria Police, posed in South Shields sunshine in May 1995. Its medium-width stripe was enhanced, as many came to be, by a further low stripe of checks. Any car loses a degree of its elegance with such additions, but the fine lines shine through here, and the Northumbria badge is always one to gladden the heart. The Met bought scores of this model, in the fastback version. (PC)

Banana Splits?

If a red stripe is a jam sandwich, what should we call a yellow one? Many forces used the standard stripe for some length of time before making a change. The most obvious and popular alternative was to replace the red or orange, which could fade badly, with yellow, which suffered less, or less obviously at least.

Hampshire was one force to make the crossover and the results were undoubtedly smart. Since more variety was involved, who could find fault? On this BMW 525 E12, the Hampshire practice of breaking the stripe at the front door, and using that for POLICE titling and the force badge, is plainly on view.

A Mark I 800 series fastback Rover of Avon & Somerset Constabulary parades its yellow livery, following use of the standard. The cut-out for the force badge is matched by one associated with the filler cap, as it was found that spilt fuel would quickly discolour and degrade striping of any colour. Also noteworthy is the red checking at the rear. Many forces employed rear red checks of all sizes in the pre-chevron era. (JO)

A similar 827 of Cheshire Constabulary sports a narrower stripe and a rather splendid 'bucket' light as it rests at the police post at Knutsford Services on the M6. (BCC)

Rather more numerous in service than the Mk V, the Mk IV (or XJ40 version of the XJ6) had its problems but was generally popular when it was 'up together'. Despite lacking the aesthetic advantages of the Mk V, this Derbyshire example looks rather fine with its generous mid-height wide stripe and equally ample force badge. Not too bad an office, many thought. (BCC)

Small Bananas

Small cars within fleets were in general slower to receive striping than their front-line cousins and, when they got it, it tended to be more basic. Sometimes the lesser vehicles would get no force badge.

This example defies at least two of those generalisations. A Kent Constabulary Escort III 1.6, it was almost obsessively dressed with most panels edged on all sides. Of outstanding note is that (rare for the time) considerable thought had gone into the frontal aspect, with a bold panel and titling, whereas many forces' motorway and traffic cars showed no identification whatsoever. (JOC)

Just as with the last example, this '95 West Yorkshire Police Astra III had a more sophisticated lightbar than vehicles in its category might usually have expected to have had. Astras, like the Escort, will have worn most of the UK livery variations ever invented over the course of their long production runs. As this shot makes clear, the outer edging stripes used by West Yorkshire Police for some years were actually dark green. (PC)

Isuzu was one of the competitors for the Land Rover company in the 90s. This Durham Trooper wears a simple yellow stripe, except that it's neither. The force frequently used gold in place of Saturn Yellow, usually with a double band. Close inspection reveals a smart compound stripe with reflective bands outside the blue edge stripes. Durham vehicles in the glory days carried an exceptionally confident statement of ownership. (JO)

After a long period when Warwickshire's non-traffic vehicles used the standard sandwich, the force seemed to succumb to propaganda that implied that red was bad and yellow was good. This was odd since the force's very, very red traffic livery was one of the highest visible ever. The replacement scheme seen on this Peugeot 306 was smart enough and fairly distinctive, with its generous widths of blue. (JO)

Early Doors

A minor tradition involved confining livery almost entirely to the front doors of a vehicle. This created a small category of rather disparate vehicles over time, not readily fitting into any other category.

This scheme can be described as California Highway Patrol without the white roof. It was taken up by Devon Constabulary not long before the force was amalgamated with Exeter City for fourteen months only, prior to the further amalgamation with Cornwall and the City of Plymouth. The arms are those of Devon County Council. Ford's Mk III Zephyr 6 looked purposeful from the front, impressive from the rear and fairly ugly in profile. (JOC)

Following a nine-year love affair with DayGlo orange, Lancashire traffic livery reverted in 1974 to white with just two blue flashes for white titling on the rear wings. Motorway Range Rovers were allowed orange doors. They also received matt-black bonnets to reduce the sun's glare reflecting into crews' eyes. (PM Photography, Ken Porter)

The Vauxhall Chevette had been one of the many types to join the panda ranks. Both Essex and Southend pandas had been all white, not using the familiar scheme. This represents then a first foray into marking the small car fleet with anything other than a badge or POLICE vinyls. It was a solution that became regular in Essex for a while and found some traction elsewhere, notably with British Transport Police. (PM Photography)

A variety of similar door-only schemes became fairly common, Norfolk Constabulary fielding this one seen on a Ford Fiesta in King's Lynn in 1991. (BH)

The Lows and Highs of Striping

Livery could be applied at varying heights, thereby increasing the permutations and opportunities for individuality. Pictured are two views of cars of the same type:

On the 1978/9 Rover SD1 of Hertfordshire, the stripe has been applied at an unusually low level. Clearly it was a decision taken by workshops on a model-by-model basis as on the Range Rover parked alongside the high option has been taken. This picture affords a good view of a boot-mounted POLICE STOP sign of the era, developed to avoid the wind resistance associated with roof boxes and carefully designed for the minimal space available with a fastback. (JOC)

The 1985/6 Cambridge car is post-facelift (recognisable by the extended bumpers) but essentially the same body to be treated. In this case, the high option has been taken. The profile view demonstrates that it was the right decision, certainly for that width of stripe. Positioning any lower would have involved cut-outs for the wheel arches, which would have significantly diminished its impact and effectiveness. (Norman Tarling)

The Thin Blue Line

The application of livery involved costs, which some forces initially were reluctant to incur. Those that did used livery initially for vehicles most likely to be in vulnerable positions – effectively motorway and traffic cars. No one saw any necessity to afford the same protection to lesser vehicles; they were, after all, now mainly white and had police signs – some even had blue beacons. Job done! Inevitably, however, such cars and vans could find themselves in hazardous situations, and attention turned to affordable ways of enhancing their presence. The most basic was to provide them with a minimal sidestripe in the form of one strip of reflective tape – a thin blue line.

This 1978/9 Morris Marina illustrates Thames Valley Constabulary's somewhat wobbly solution. The police use of patrol cars like Marinas and Avengers was almost enough to end a lifelong interest in police vehicles for the present writer. Fortunately things improved and their memory has become just another episode. (PM Photography, Ken Porter)

Devon & Cornwall Constabulary's considerable fleets of Escorts and Fiestas were equally treated to a single line. Coupled with the attractive force arms and force titling incorporated in the stripe, the effect was surprisingly stylish. (Norman Tarling)

Worth the Wait

When in 1977 the Metropolitan Police finally made the decision to adopt a sidestripe, the result was surprisingly good. That an affordable scheme could yet be distinctive and befit the nation's capital was a major achievement. It did enjoy the advantage of being paired with the force's splendid coat of arms, granted in September 1967. The stripe avoided the widely used jam-sandwich and mustard-sandwich forms by omitting blue – a sound decision. Instead it employed three equal, medium strips of red/gold/red, the combination giving the hint of class appropriate for a leading city. The independent City of London force, operating at the heart of the Met's territory, had been using stripes for some five years, but had never, nor would ever, find a scheme to quite equal the Met's first for panache and style.

The Rover SD1 shows the stripe in a mid position, contrasting with the two provincial examples just seen. (PM Photography, Ken Porter)

This Metro picture shows that the same stripe exactly was applied throughout the fleet. It also highlights another belated decision, responding to the fact that panda cars could often be found in situations where a blue beacon could enhance safety. Pandas in some places were wired so that beacons could only be used when the vehicle was stationary, to discourage involvement in pursuits and high-speed response. This measure reportedly resulted largely in an epidemic of flat batteries at incidents.

Budget Lines

Elsewhere, striping could show evidence of tight budget allocations for livery. This Ford Cortina IV was a traffic car in Cumbria, but its markings are exceptionally minimal for a front-line car.

It was predictable that panda types might receive more modest striping, and this North Yorkshire Fiesta fulfilled those expectations. Thanks to wear and tear, it is revealed that the stripe could easily have been wider, had not the decision been made to apply the blue tape *over* the red as opposed to alongside it, at no extra cost other than that of a little more fitting round door handles. (JOC)

White is Alright

It can be argued that an all-white vehicle could be safer than one decked out in blocks of contrasting colours. We should remind ourselves of some instances where forces persisted with them.

But, first, a reminder of the pre-stripe era when white was king. In 1966, as this line-up was being photographed in Chichester, not far away in East Sussex stripes were being invented, and would soon appear on MGB GTs. However, this is West Sussex and *its* Bs will avoid coloured tape until amalgamation. Also lined-up are one of the force's celebrated Mk I Lotus-Cortinas and two perennial stalwarts. Every formation in England and Wales will have run at least the odd Minivan and Land Rover, and many ran fleets of them. The Mini made an ideal single dog van, among numerous other roles – including that of panda alongside its saloon counterpart. Land Rovers filled every tasking from motorways to rural patrol to pulling incident trailers and exhibition caravans. This was a Series IIA and looks brand new. (EMB)

Twenty years later and rather fewer miles to the west, Hampshire Constabulary was still putting plain-white area cars into service and would continue to do so for a further six years or so. The force had maintained a long relationship with the Volvo marque; the 240 PS (Police Special) gave good service and was well liked. (JO)

In sunny North Wales, the police happily ran all-white beat cars. After operating Minis much later than any other fleet, buying them until 1987/8, the force had the choice of numerous so-called superminis for a replacement and the Peugeot 205 was one of the European offerings tried. All-white Vauxhall Corsas would be bought as late as the 93/4 model year. (JOC)

At the other margin of the principality and even later in time, white IRVs or incident response vehicles could look quite businesslike. Good emergency lighting plays a major role in vehicle presence and safety, and so it is interesting to see one 1997 Gwent Constabulary Astra III unit equipped with additional high intensity reds and one not. (PC)

Checking Out the Fleets

One step beyond a single blue stripe is a line of checks.

A line doesn't come any narrower than this Hertfordshire dressing from 1990. There are actually three rows of the smallest checks found in the archive. The Escort was widely used, but this shot highlights a rare feature in depicting a patrol car with a sunroof. This was a batch of superseded cars with pre-fitted options, bought at a bargain price at model update time. (BH)

Checks you can actually *see* are found in this shot of a Northamptonshire unit. It's a Mk IV Escort again, two-door and with black and white checks, two rows but larger, and black instead of blue. The effect is crisp and the force's Tudor Rose badge helps the cause. It would later be replaced by a ridiculous logo.

Going Up. Similar-sized checks but more rows give a wider band on this Dyfed-Powys Police Maestro. Potentially the Maestro was a better car than it is probably given credit for – the MG version was a great drive. The prospect of spending your career in cars like the Austin would hardly do much to boost recruitment. It's a beautiful area to work, however. (PC)

And Up. The number of rows is down again but size is larger, so overall it is a much bolder scheme, in black – one that Gloucestershire Constabulary was happy to replicate on area cars such as Sierras. This earlier Escort, a Mk III, was captured during a driver-training run on a refreshment stop at Staverton Airport. (PC)

The permutations seem endless as the row count drops and the size steps up again. This is Lincolnshire and beyond the L-reg VE64 Transit bus is the interesting sight of an Astra III with the same stripe, but set as low as you would ever have seen on that model anywhere, I should imagine. (JO)

There's nothing shy about the application on this Cheshire Astra II. It looks to be much the same size as Gloucestershire's, but it isn't quite so grabbing. Could it be that the checks aren't black but very dark blue? A helpful notice tells us that the setting is Macclesfield. (BCC)

An earlier Transit, a VE6 from 1987/88, demonstrates a very little-known livery for second-tier vehicles in North Yorkshire. Three rows of medium checks are enclosed by a full border of matching stripes. The only question is 'matching what?' but I think the answer, once again, is very dark blue. (JO)

The only counterpart, I believe, is South Wales Police's scheme for similar units, in which two lines of red checks were topped and tailed by red stripes, which I imagine all came printed on the same roll integrated with the checks. The arrangement is seen here on an Astra IV and is in good condition, but this was a livery that did not wear well. Apart from the usual fading associated with red, this tape would suffer in the car washer, with the red bleeding into the white and turning the stripe into a nasty-looking wound – not a good look. In fact the process can be seen starting on the rear door. (PC)

Sandwich Fillings

This brings us to another combination that provided some exceptionally smart liveries. In this group, checks were bordered by red bands.

A Cleveland Constabulary Cavalier II from *circa* 1983 provides the first example, which the force used for around ten years up to the mid-1980s. Note that the black lowerworks, fashionable at the time, leave not a great deal of bodywork available for striping and signage.

Not too far away to the west, Cumbria Constabulary's very similar arrangement was slightly bolder overall, with more prominent outer bands. The force had used more conventional schemes earlier, but stayed with this one, also for about ten years. It moved on only around 1990. (BCC)

Cleveland's neighbour, North Yorkshire Police, used another such livery for at least seventeen years to 1996. With proportionally thinner outer stripes, it was perhaps the sharpest version of the three. Another Cavalier shot, of a Mk III, underlines the popularity of that model during the Golden Age. North Yorkshire's badge at the time, with the white rose of Yorkshire as its centrepiece, could appear blank. This was rectified in later redesigns. (JOC)

Two North Yorkshire Police assets lay over at a small town station, probably Helmsley, in May 1995. Note that lower orders of vehicles got two rows of checks instead of the traffic unit's three. Both vehicles suffer from the empty-badge syndrome. These two units are not the first in the book so far to display POLICE in reversed letters on the bonnet, but they are the boldest. The actual value of reversing the letters is questionable, but the practice adds yet another aspect of individuality to be enjoyed. (PC)

Reverse Gear

Two forces used a form of reversed hybrid livery, with a thin blue stripe bisecting a full-width red or orange stripe.

This brand-new Scorpio demonstrator, seen being handed over to Lancashire Constabulary's traffic department, has clearly been striped more for style than safety. However, it demonstrates the principle and looks enticing, even if the Scorpio *wasn't* particularly, if crews' memories can be believed – which they usually can. (NDC)

A better impression can be gained from the humble Astramax dog van, whose repaired front wing incidentally gives an idea of how the orange reflective was prone to fading. Whereas the Scorpio's badge is traditional, that on the van has been revised to include a mission statement CARING FOR THE COUNTY on the circlet; it's thought this is the only time such a move has been made on an actual force badge in England and Wales. May it be the last. (ND)

Thames Valley Police employed this reversed stripe for all vehicles except traffic, area and ARV (Armed Response) for some twelve years until 2002. Until 1993, as can be seen, beat cars carried no force badge or force titling, which was surprising, but the arrangement was extremely smart. In that year a 'corporate' style with a shield and bold titling replaced POLICE on the doors, and so branding went from zero to full-on. (PC)

Thames valley's vehicle badge history was rather eccentric, with none used before 1972/3, when the force arms appeared on traffic cars. Commercial types had to wait, but still were given badges before the beat cars, as this 1990/1 Escort dog van proves. (Malcolm Cheshire)

Tiger, Tiger 1

While West Midland Police's normal livery showed consistent commitment to the standard jam-sandwich scheme, something more attention-grabbing was felt necessary for the force's major contribution to policing the Midlands motorways. Various groupings of forces joined together for this purpose at different times but, whatever the group, West Mids was always in it by virtue of its territory or 'ground' being at the heart of the network.

The outcome was the tiger stripe, and no vehicles wore it with more pizzazz than the Jaguar XJ6s, here represented by a Mark IV aka XJ40, actually parked under the M6 at the motorway base at Perry Barr. Note that no force badge is visible, but then, with that livery, can there be any doubt? Well, yes, there can, actually. (BCC)

A 2001 Volvo V70 does carry a West Mids badge in a side window, but its main badge is of the CMPG, outside whose premises it stands. When saloon cars were deemed not suitable for traffic work, there were really just two main contenders – the V70 and the BMW 5 series Touring (estate to us), with a few forces taking the Mercedes C or E class estates. Note the roof numerals for the force helicopter, 20. If there is any doubt and you can see those, you will know the vehicle is a West Midlands asset. (MH)

And here's why there might be confusion.

Even enthusiasts can get this wrong at times. At first glance, two classic Range Rovers wear the same livery. But they don't. The nearer unit belonged to West Mercia Constabulary and its tiger stripes ran in exactly the opposite directions to the West Midlands unit parked beyond it. The key: West Mercia's stripes suggest an arch or a hill, while West Midlands's a valley or a depression – no offence to the Birmingham area. The extra depth of the tigers and the yellow grille are West Midland giveaways. Actually, Essex Police also used yellow grilles on the Range Rover, but confusion isn't likely in that case. (CT)

This early application of tiger stripes to a West Mercia Mk I Rover 800 series could perhaps do with some extra depth but, in truth, the effect is not bad, enhancing the lines of what was far from the finest design to come out of the English Midlands. West Mercia was and is a partner in the CMPG. (CT)

A fifteen-minute drive on the M5 southbound from Worcester and the West Mercia HQ and Gloucestershire is reached; so, when in around 1994 that county had identified the need for a new motorway and traffic livery, the force didn't have far to look for inspiration.

Four examples of the result, actually two traffic cars and two ARVs, are seen at the Bamfurlong traffic base, just off the M5. The stripes on the 850 T5s may be compared with the previous standard livery, which continued for area cars and all other units ... (PC)

... as seen at Churchdown police station, where a divisional traffic Cavalier V6 sits beside a Rover 400 area car. Notable on the latter is a Gloucestershire speciality, the reflective check tape on the front valance. While forces give great attention to side markings and rear high-vis, little thought has traditionally gone into making cars conspicuous from the front. The valance tape was remarkably effective and was a rare move in the right direction. (PC)

Go north on the M6 from Birmingham and you are soon through Staffordshire, and then it's Cheshire, another constabulary with proud traditions, no better represented by the tiger livery that the force introduced around 1993.

Cheshire's tigers, as carried by this facelifted BMW 525i E34, were topped and tailed by slim rows of double checks. Arguably the best-looking BMW ever, with the livery at its high point where it included both the terrific coat of arms and neat force titling – what could be better? Sunshine too. (BCC)

More sunshine at Capenhurst, shared by an Astravan dog unit. To some extent the writing was on the wall, or on the door anyway, for shortly the arms would be deleted from cars in favour of the written identification seen on the van. (PC)

It's so important that such images of the glory days have been captured for posterity. Beyond the Cheshire Astra can be seen another fine livery, now also history; that of the Atomic Energy Authority Constabulary.

Tiger, Tiger 3

In essence, Hampshire's tigers amounted to a jam sandwich, with the jam filling changed to red and white. The white was highly reflective; so much so that it was necessary to add the yellow car outline to show the reflection was coming from a car and not a signboard. The extra row of checks was standard fare by the time this livery was rolling out in 1997, as the following pages will disclose. Like most mission statements, Hampshire's thankfully indecipherable scrawl across the bonnet drew plenty of adverse comment.

Two tigers make a chevron, which was the basis of Lancashire Constabulary's final motorway livery, introduced in 1994. Chevron supporters argue that, with a vehicle parked in the ideal fend-off position at a traffic incident, the chevrons will indicate which direction traffic should head to avoid obstructions. This takes no account of occasions when it might be impossible to park in an ideal position, leaving chevrons indicating a dangerous course of action, rather than a safe one.

This BMW 3 series E36 served on the Isle of Wight, where the duties of traffic and area car were combined. It is caught at Bembridge Airport. Although the tiger stripes are supposed to run as seen on this vehicle, and in the opposite direction to those of Cheshire, when first being applied several mistakes were made, including cars being outshopped with the striping correct on one side and wrong on the other. (PC)

The Lancashire chevron livery was especially bold when applied to the Volvo estate, but certainly eye-catching on whatever vehicle it adorned. In this application, the originator chose to pick out the shape of the car, much as Hampshire did in yellow, here with a strip of checks.

Manchester Musings

Greater Manchester's final individual livery included a tiger stripe, hence the inclusion here of its predecessor. That reflected the American-led trend to pay consultants to create 'corporate identity', ignoring the facts that police forces are not companies and had perfectly good iconography, born of practicality and long tradition. This misplaced quest for an updated image could see, at worst, designers' flights of fancy, decorating vehicles as if they were cigarette packets or toothpaste cartons. Often their purpose, and the practical, safety aspects of the markings they carry, could be totally forgotten. GMP's 1997/8 scheme was only slightly chocolate box and designer-esque – actually quite attractive. Other forces would spend good public money to much less effect.

At the very time that the 'National Police Livery' of Battenburg blocks was beginning to infest the nation, GMP went through its second major corporate image exercise inside six years. That included yet another new livery for non-traffic vehicles. Like Lancashire's chevrons, the basic colours were blue and yellow, responding to a jobsworthian proposal that all European police vehicles should be so liveried. The colours effectively formed a sidestripe made up of rather chopped-off tiger stripes. It was infinitely preferable to the all-conquering national scheme and lasted well into the 2010s.

GMP's corporate sidestripe had seven elements, six of them very thin and wispy when seen close-up. It somewhat lacked the robust look of previous stripes, while incorporating the force name diminished the size of the POLICE title, which would surely have been better across the lower doors, as seen in examples on previous pages. This Mondeo II served at Manchester Airport, as can be seen from the yellow roof and the amber airside beacon mounted atop the standard Premier Hazard lightbar. (ND)

The 2003 redesign included a dark-blue roof, almost a nod towards tradition, with a length of check band as a dividing line. Also present were a tidy force identification; a reworked force badge in which the designer had dared to tamper with the Royal Cypher (surely a treasonable act?); and a four-word mission statement in the place where sense dictates the message POLICE should be writ large.

The cost of two image makeovers must have been eye-watering. No doubt the cost of the second livery saved money compared to Battenburg and it was more attractive, but then so was the previous scheme.

Double Standards

It can be interesting to note how forces using some distinctive types of livery are situated geographically and to speculate as to why they might be linked. The following group is found mainly in Wales and North-West England.

Having used very much standard markings, in 1990 Merseyside Police adopted a new livery of two medium bands of green and blue, with a similar-width space between. At the same time a new version of the force badge, featuring those same two colours, was introduced. The effect was smart and quite unlike anything previously seen in the UK.

The new livery was not particularly high-vis and many front-line units received a very substantial yellow band on their lower flanks, which rather diminished the stylish look. This Cavalier carried POLICE STOP boxes at both front and rear, signalling the change of policy regarding the stopping of vehicles, which was now to be from behind.

Not all vehicles received the yellow addition. As an ARV, recognisable by the roof symbol, this Senator Mk II did without – and looked rather better for it. It sizzled in the sun at Smithdown Lane police station in Liverpool in June 1998. (PC)

Four years later, nearby North Wales Police unveiled a new livery with lessons clearly learned from the Merseyside experience. As it was there, the basic striping was the same throughout the fleet. The principal difference saw the two stripes more closely spaced – neater, if less attention-getting. The scheme involved a shaped cut-out for the force badge and some small force titling towards the rear. Sadly no scheme would enhance the Vauxhall Corsa, which looked ungainly from any angle. (MHC)

The reason for the closer spacing is clear on this traffic unit, where two bands of checks were added to give a seriously compound stripe. Merseyside yellow panels were added, in addition to some front and rear yellow chevrons. Pretty it wasn't, but it *was* interesting. Traffic cars got a decently sized POLICE sign on the bonnet. It actually reads HEDDLU, which is strange, given that 'constabulary' is held to be potentially confusing and inaccessible – whereas 'heddlu' apparently is not.

It is astonishing to look at these cars, especially the jazzy Mondeo, and to compare them with vehicles that were pictured earlier, tasked to patrol the same roads some sixty years previously.

Second Double Standards

North Wales's southern and far-flung neighbour, Dyfed-Powys Police, also broke away from its traditional liveries in the mid-1990s and adopted the Merseyside style, emulating the latter's stripe exactly, but in blue over red. The scheme wisely substituted a band of checks in place of acres of yellow on the lower flanks. The Rover 200 was a pretty car and could have become a new Minor 1000, had the company not fallen into the wrong hands. (Colin Dunford)

To capture the essence of the Golden Age, one-offs and oddities have been avoided in favour of what was once everyday and typical. An exception is the upside-down scheme seen on this DPP car in Lampeter, which has been included because it shows a variation on a livery that's both mysterious and attractive. It also had a silver middle stripe instead of plain-white paintwork, and other minor changes that give an extra smart look. The reason has yet to be explained. (BCC)

Nothing is currently known about this Humberside Range Rover from about 1982. It could be a one-off but, if it is, let it represent the fact that the Golden Age was a time of great experimentation with liveries, vehicles and practices. (JOC)

Durham Constabulary was the longest and best known practitioner of double striping. These were full-edged double sidestripes, or nearly full double on this 2003 Mercedes E-Class ARV example. In yellow or gold, and with definitive force identification, Durham blazed the trail for bold individual liveries from 1987 and held out against the pressure for nationwide mediocrity longer than most. (PC)

Capital Growth

As the 90s were approaching, London's Met Police decided a bolder livery was needed for traffic vehicles, and a new compound stripe was introduced.

Essentially the previous stripe was broadened and a border of reflective blue was introduced top, bottom and each end, giving five strong lines where there had been three lesser ones. With the force arms and a POLICE panel, the impact was very much enhanced, as can be seen. (CT)

It was not long before the superb coat of arms was peeled off the entire fleet and replaced by a piece of graphic work so poor that it is an embarrassment to our capital city. Happily, everything else about the Omega I looks good, and it is included here to show the lower reflective panel and its bold POLICE graphic, which was the next addition to the basic scheme. (PC)

A year or so after the launch of the traffic livery, a slightly reduced version arrived for area cars and other categories. Its proportions varied over time, but one example is seen on this 2002 Ford Focus. The car is silver, following a trend, as colours other than white fared better in the second-hand market – an important factor for police vehicles, which are sold on relatively young, if they survive to their mileage limit.

Cars now carried their air numbers – their roof identification for force helicopters – on their rear flanks, while the badge, while still using the same execrable rendering of the force arms, had been redesigned with the vinyl incorporating a mission statement of typical vacuity and near-illegibility.

On borrowed time, image-wise, this BMW 530d E60 ARV exhibited further subtle developments. Livery elements were now computer designed and came in kits specific to models, and their individual contours. Note the revised mission statement. On the arrival of Ian Blair from Surrey to be Met Commissioner, the expensive vinyls reading 'Working for a safer London' had been junked to be replaced by 'Working together for a safer London'. How gratifying to see public money so well spent.

Something of the City

The City of London's first livery appeared in 1971/2, more than five years before its mighty neighbour followed suit. It was a standard blue/yellow/blue stripe, but that was later upgraded with a further band of large checks. These, however, were red, and the combination, as seen on this pre-facelift Granada II Estate, was not a comfortable one. (PM Photography, Ken Porter)

Losing the checks, changing the stripe and revising the badge with some neat if rather small force titling restored some of the good taste appropriate for a force policing London's square mile. Just don't mention the wheels on this Granada III. The 140 mph car (theoretically able to traverse the force area in around 27 seconds) is here seen at Heathrow to escort one of the regular gold-bullion runs in and out of the nation's financial hub. (CT)

The livery would eventually settle down to the quite-acceptable hybrid scheme seen on this Mondeo II. Worthy of note are the air numbers on the boot lid of a saloon (a practice shared with Essex) and the CITY POLICE titling. No need to qualify which city as, in the amalgamations of 1974, all remaining proud city forces in England and Wales were swept away on the grounds that they could not possibly be efficient. One might wonder how the City of London force escaped the same fate.

The CITY POLICE vinyl had a mercurial character, sometimes appearing, sometimes not. It is actually featured on the bonnet of this Vectra, which was one of the last cars to wear proper livery. The final iteration of the city colours saw the bold POLICE title across the lower doors. (ND)

Sussex – Avenger to Avensis

Sussex, in my view, used two of the most handsome combinations ever for their sidestripes.

The original East Sussex-designed red/red/red was used by Sussex Constabulary and through the 1974 name change until about 1980. This Avenger (by now it was a Talbot) must, therefore, be one of the earliest new vehicles to be dressed in this second livery. As the extra beacons for airside demonstrate, this unit worked at Gatwick Airport, which was policed by Surrey until the 1974 upheavals. (PM Photography, Ken Porter)

Sussex Police's red bands were generally broader than others, but there were exceptions, as on these Metros at Rye, which are almost City of London-like in appearance. Note that the car on the right carries the old Royal Cypher badge, while that on the left wears the new badge with the force shield. (PC)

On the A27 near Chichester is one of the stars of the Golden Age, the Volvo 850 T5. It's not beautiful but is nevertheless intensely appealing because of its supremely purposeful air. (PC)

How thing have changed. When sidestripes were being dreamt up in East Sussex, no foreign-manufactured police car patrolled British roads. When one did it provoked uproar, or the newspapers did. Thirty-four years later, most patrol cars were from overseas. A Sussex officer hoses off his area car – a 2000 Toyota Avensis.

Not What You Think

The livery and badge suggest Sussex, while the Taunton registration and the blue-and-yellow-striped Range Rover prompt thoughts of Avon & Somerset. A&S did look at red/yellow/red experimentally while transitioning from blue/red/blue to blue/yellow/blue, but that was around 1988. The answer is that this was a Cheshire Constabulary scheme, adopted for only three years or so at the turn of the 1990s after blue/yellow/blue and before the coming of the tiger stripes. (JOC)

This Surrey Police livery seems to be a complex one – a compound of five stripes akin to that of the neighbouring Met. It is and it isn't. There is a central reflective strip down the middle of the main red/orange band, but it is essentially the same colour as the band and so only shows up under some light conditions, more so in photographs. Normally it seems to be a standard blue/red/blue. The weak force titling is absurd and unfit for purpose, an example of a trend mentioned earlier. The significance of the incy-wincy squares may only be guessed at.

Going back in time Surrey-wise, the explanation becomes clearer: the reflective bonus strip is near the top here, but the fading of the main strip has made its presence clearer. The rather better force titling on the door suffers, in daylight at least, by being blue on a red background. What a classic shape the Senator II was: great from every angle. How could the same company produce that Corsa?

The nearly contemporary IRV reinforces the picture on a gloomy day. The door and bonnet show the excellent force identity and frontal message thrown away by the designer of the corporate image opposite (and those who commissioned and accepted the so-called improvement). (PM Photography)

Waffles in Red

A good number of forces realised that the basic jam sandwich could be enhanced at night by the substitution of reflective checks for the blue outline tape. In the absence of any official or habitual name, we will call these schemes waffles.

Northamptonshire Police predictably plumped for the black-and-white variety – a sound decision, giving a sharp look to this 1986/7 Ford Sierra. (JOC)

Blue and white was of course the alternative, and that was the tape used to good effect on Hertfordshire's fleet, including many a Senator II. The picture demonstrates that rear-end high-vis was held to be very important with many fast roads and, of course, motorways in a county that had lost several vehicles in serious rear-end shunts.

Gwent Constabulary went the same way as Northamptonshire, but used somewhat smaller checks and thinner bands to less effect. The Volvo was a 940 Estate, forerunner of the mighty 850 T5. Please excuse the intrusion of the interloper parked adjacent. (PC)

Traditional midsize station vans became progressively rarer as larger PSU-style (Police Support Unit) vehicles took over the duty in many towns, while elsewhere smaller vehicles like the Cub or the Transit Connect with prisoner cages could do the job. Cambridgeshire nevertheless bought the LDV Pilot in 1997/8 and dressed it, as with their cars, with the red-and-black waffle.

Waffles in Red 2

The value of the check tape and the extra reflection from the white is beautifully demonstrated in this fine night shot by a unknown photographer. The picture of a Greater Manchester Pegasus Range Rover highlights the vector (V) light bar, which offers superior visibility for drivers to either side, and so is safer at crossroads and many other situations. Also seen are the extra blue lights set in the grille, which is in traditional GMP orange. Crews called these vehicles 'the jeeps'.

Like its neighbour Gwent, South Wales Police did not follow the other two modern Welsh forces in adopting the double stripe. Indeed, the SWP livery was remarkably similar to Gwent's, although this 3 Series BMW E36 enjoys yellow lower panels and chevrons in a rather pleasing scheme. (Fire Fotos, Ken Reid)

The Derbyshire Constabulary 850 T5 has a wider stripe than most in the group. Its noteworthy feature is the round blue spotlight-like repeater mounted in the centre of the grille, which was a feature of most Derbyshire and Nottinghamshire cars in the Golden Era. (PC)

Last in the group is Norfolk Constabulary, which chose the blue-and-white option. The back of the Mondeo II is an attractive design, enhanced by Norfolk's pre-chevron high-vis additions. Notable is the use of the car as a mobile billboard for the DVLA. (JOC)

The bodies of police vehicles would become increasingly used for, or littered with, mission statements, exhortations such as 'If You Drink, Don't Drive', telephone numbers, web addresses, sponsorship stickers, Crimestoppers logos and vinyls promoting anti-crime incentives, drives or programmes. Merseyside Police would regularly use the convenient yellow skirts for such purposes, as well as to denote special-purpose units such as the Vehicle Crime Group.

Waffles in Yellow

Lincolnshire Constabulary turned to the yellow sidestripe with blue check edging for traffic cars only in around 1997/8, after years with red and then yellow sandwiches. Other types of unit followed later. The force is believed to have been the only one in the country to run the Rover 45. How popular the 400 was with crews is unknown but it was attractive-looking, and the 45 was an even more beguiling development. The demise of Rover was a great British tragedy. (PC)

Essex Constabulary. Ditto as regards the stripe. The AMC Jeep looked reasonable and went well enough on the road, although it was no Range Rover or Discovery off. Reports say it was seriously expensive to run in the UK, and so there were no volume users lining up. Two are posed outside the long-time Essex HQ, Springfield Court, at Chelmsford. (JOC)

The competition. Matchless all round but, as it went up-market, the price of the Range Rover became a real disincentive, even with the substantial discounts available to police fleets. This P38A or Pegasus example patrolled Avon & Somerset and is seen at Almondsbury Motorway Base. (PC)

Through the Golden Age, Wiltshire Constabulary sampled an enormous number of vehicles. The force likes to try Honda products because the manufacturer has a facility at Swindon. This CR-V sported the blue waffle, a Crimestoppers logo and the mission statement, and yet still looked good. Bonus features were the fleet number (police vehicles should be obliged to carry simpler ID, now that VRMs are no longer readily memorable) and the emphasis given to the bonnet sign, although it could be much bolder still. (PC)

Optional Extras

Forces, as we have seen, were rightly moved to enhance their basic livery in the cause of making vehicles more readily visible, and therefore less likely to be run into. Some examples follow.

With or without a red stripe and blue lights, this Escort RS ww would automatically turn heads, but Humberside Police, not wanting its prize piece of kit written off by someone avoiding a rubbernecker, wisely fitted an extra stripe of macho checks. Actually, this was standard practice with the force traffic and ARV units, but it was a good excuse to feature the RS. (BCC)

South Yorkshire Police had used a standard sandwich and badge, before giving vehicles a new badge with a mediaeval ribbon bearing a dubious mission statement. The upside was new force titling that was bold and clear, slightly Australian in feel. The Senator is featured thanks to the extra check band and the unusual rear chevron pattern. The notice on the side of the motorway post at Woodhall services bears inappropriate and thoroughly ineffective graphics, which were about to be inflicted on the entire fleet. They won't appear in this book. (PC)

There's no denying that this Devon & Cornwall Constabulary Range Rover grabbed attention in a big way, which was the idea. It appears to have ticked all the boxes, but come back and look at it later, when you've read the brief guide to the science behind high-vis. (ND)

There were no problems with the Dorset Skoda Octavia, included in this section by dint of its large POLICE on the doors. It has the purple badge redesign, a surefire recognition feature – and frontal awareness. Dorset's check striping always looked different, as it well might because in daylight it was *grey* and blue. Was this perhaps to limit excessively dazzling reflection from white at night? (MH)

Not many Austin Maestros would have carried grown-up stripes and extra checks, but this Lincolnshire car did. It was reputedly the last Maestro in service there when it was pictured at an ambulance event in September 1995. A Lincolnshire habit was the mounting of small POLICE STOP boxes, which projected beyond the bumpers front and rear. You have to speculate about their survival rate. (PC)

The elevated roof of the Land Rover Discovery offered the bonus of adding more hi-vis. The Thames Valley workshops took full advantage when preparing them as motorway-accident tenders. Crews were not enthusiastic about the choice of the diesel-engined version for this high-profile work as virtually every other car and van on the road could pass a Disco even when it was flat out 'on the blues'. (Geraint Roberts)

When applying livery to the original-shape Discovery, high and medium options were available for the main stripe. This facelifted V8 model shows Humberside Police's preference for the high position, and the bonus checks were a regular feature as we have seen. (JO)

Suffolk Constabulary's scheme on this Mk I Mondeo has a basic feel about it and the black-and-white checks are a useful addition. One can understand, perhaps, why the force livery was shortly to be updated. Suffolk long favoured mounting the force badge on the rear doors, joining Thames Valley, Warwickshire and others in the practice. (JOC)

Other Colours Were Available

Down the whole history of British police transport, interest has always come from vehicles that did not conform to the expected colour norms of the time. Here is a small selection.

In the last days of the West Riding Constabulary, before it absorbed six city and borough forces and was renamed West Yorkshire Constabulary, it took the surprising move of introducing some all-yellow traffic cars. The Vauxhall Cresta PC was a barge, much like its contemporary, the Ford Zephyr IV; neither was popular with crews. The Vauxhall found very few police buyers. The smaller Victor 3.3 was also run in yellow by the force.

Special-purpose units sometimes have livery wholly different from the host force scheme. The Met took such a decision when forming the Diplomatic Protection Group in 1974. A unit set up to provide (initially) discreetly armed officers to protect embassies and other diplomatic and government premises, its transport requirements were for response cars to patrol the appropriate areas and for personnel carriers to permit shift change and rotation of officers. Both types are caught in this view at a force open day. (CT)

The trend for orange-and-white motorway-accident units was begun by Lancashire. Thames Valley Police followed with a series of units over the years when it became responsible for a section of the M1 way north of London, beyond the Hertfordshire and Bedfordshire sections, plus growing lengths of the M4 from just west of Heathrow and the Met's ground. (PM Photography, Ken Porter)

A reminder of those forces that resisted white vans and persisted with blue. Lancashire was one, and this Leyland Daf City is finished in a particularly pleasant shade. The attractive picture belies the fact that the Sherpa was heartily disliked by many officers, particularly if it was allocated after a spell using Transits. (JOC)

Mix and Match

Hertfordshire's panda cars appear not to have had the normal white element to the livery, and the light blue seems to have given way to dark fairly quickly. Thereafter pandas and section cars appeared over a long timespan in standard manufacturers' shades, eventually with standard jam sidestripes and the county shield of arms. The Escort IV here was caught at the time of the introduction of the replacement force badge, as can be seen from the outgoing arms on the traffic car parked alongside. (Norman Tarling)

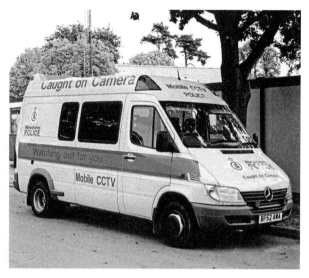

CCTV units are essentially PSU carriers, offering an extra deterrent to bad behaviour. It was realised that a distinctive and stand-out livery would advertise and emphasise that capability, so such vehicles mostly appeared in variations of yellow and orange, often highly decorated and usually heavily signwritten. Few incorporated stripes, but Warwickshire was one force that did, seen to dramatic effect on this facelifted Mk I Mercedes Sprinter. (MH)

How London's Diplomatic Protection Group changed from the days of the Austin 1800 at its inception. A 2003/4 BMW 530d E39 is pictured making its way through the capital, now an avowed and fully marked ARV. The full Met livery combined gloriously with the basic paintwork. This assumes the car was actually red, for technology now enables a car to be wrapped in vinyl and run in service as a quite different colour, the vinyl peeled off for the car's resale on decommissioning. (MH)

The onrush of Battenburg would accelerate the use of silver base cars and, indeed, dark blue. Holding out against the tide for as long as possible, Leicestershire Constabulary on this BMW X5 incorporated some Battenburg add-ons, the blue outline strips, as well as some extra touches of its own, in orange. Most significant of those were the bonnet flashes to address that perennial problem of frontal markings. Probably inspired by Swiss practice, they gave the big Beemer a distinctly European look. (PC)

Time travelling back to Lancashire in 1974, when a change of policy saw bright orange cars give way to something far less attention-getting – indeed, something minimalist when compared to the jam sandwich gaining ground generally at the time. It was a strange move, which was not long-lived, but provided a unique livery style to add to the inventory. This is a Consul 3000GT, the name Granada initially being subject to a court case between Ford and the entertainment company of that name. (JOC)

Staffordshire is not a force known for newsworthy innovation on the vehicle front but, in the late 1980s, its area and general-purpose cars carried an extraordinarily distinctive scheme, with the yellow apparently painted rather than being vinyl sheet. The Escort was a favoured buy for fleet managers over most of its thirty-seven years of production, this one being a Mk IV. A clear view is afforded of the knot device on the force badge. (JOC)

Perhaps the most idiosyncratic sidestripe ever; this was a Gwent Constabulary scheme, which may have been driven by the cost of vinyl. There was, however, the cash to provide a mission statement for the door (bilingual indeed, so two of them) that was too small to read, mercifully. The standard Royal Cypher badge would shortly be replaced by a very poor graphic. (PC)

Astra IIIs again, but then they *were* one of the mainstays during the Golden Age. In 1997 two Nottinghamshire beat cars at Ollerton display that county's intriguing scheme for such units – one that was very smart if not that arresting. The white reflective band was presumably effective at night. The picture shows that the M registration year, 1994/5, saw the facelift of the original (right) to give the updated frontal look (left). (PC)

Four Four by Fours

So far this look at the Age of Enlightenment has not done justice to the full range of vehicles with off-road capability, a sector that has blossomed over the years with imports challenging the former supremacy of Land Rover company products.

Leicestershire's Isuzu Troopers were at the top end of the profile spectrum, supplying the county's four-wheel drive presence on the M1 for a number of years. The force used numerous Troopers and also bought the Vauxhall clone, the Monterey. Prominent is the force shield, which was used as an attractive stand-alone badge, before a more conventional design supplanted it.

Ford's big Explorer was found in the two rural areas of Cambridgeshire and North Yorkshire, and naturally in Essex, but it was slightly surprising to find it on duty in the Merseyside area. That said, in the 1950s the City of Liverpool had been largely and quite intensively patrolled using Land Rovers before an edict saw them withdrawn. Old hands later said that, had Land Rovers still been on the streets, the Toxteth riots would never have happened.

The Nissan Terrano could fill multiple roles at an affordable price and so found a niche with rural forces especially. Dorset Police used both it and its Ford counterpart, the Maverick. This Mk II was seen working from Blandford Forum. (MH)

The Daihatsu Fourtrak was a budget off-roader suited for rural patrol. Hampshire Constabulary bought them after Discoverys had proved costly to run. (Colin Dunford)

Not to be Left Out

In fact, dozens of interesting vehicles and great photographs have had to be omitted, to try and achieve a balance by representing as many vehicle types, forces and liveries as possible. There are plenty more for a second selection, if there is a demand. In the meantime, a few whose claims just insisted that they squeeze in.

The car that started a revolution. British industry, letter writers to *The Times* and members of parliament were all up in arms in 1966 when Hampshire Constabulary concluded that no British car on offer could match a tuned-up Volvo 221 for its combination of performance, reliability and affordability. Fortunately the chief constable was able to make the case, helped by the fact that Volvos were full of British-made components. The mould was broken, however, and overseas cars eventually became commonplace. (JO)

Knight of the road. Just as livery should help bring individuality to places, whether it's on buses, trains or police cars, heraldry does the same, bringing colour, identity and pride wherever it appears – even on dustcarts. Here the Transit III exhibits the arms originally awarded to the Norfolk Joint Police when Norwich City and Great Yarmouth Borough were merged with the county force. Few forces were content to apply a shield of arms without some explanatory titling other than POLICE, which makes pictures of Norfolk vehicles of this era quite special. (PM Photography, Ken Porter)

The Volkswagen Transporter was not the most widely used of vans, but sizeable batches bought by the Met for use as station vans, dog units and at Heathrow argue for their inclusion. This example, a T4, served Cleveland with ample role titling and a generous stripe. (BCC)

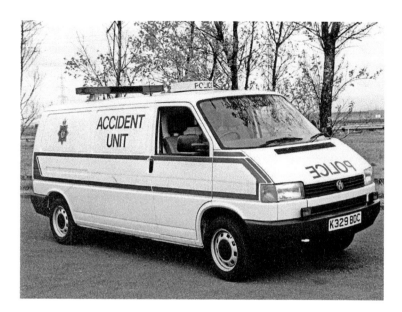

Many forces bought the Peugeot 405, so it no doubt did its job well enough. There was nothing wrong with its appearance, but it managed to be basically unexciting. That said, no force made it look more interesting than did Cheshire when its livery was at its high point. The BMW 5 Series the 405 wasn't, but the combination wasn't lacking in style. (BCC)

And Also

No survey of the heyday of police vehicles in England and Wales could omit two of the Ford Company's fondest remembered.

The 4x4 Sierra XR4 was more than good enough to take its place on the motorway network alongside the more usual classic traffic types, as seen here in the service of Bedfordshire Police. (CT)

Then there was the Sierra Sapphire Cosworth, which was happy patrolling anywhere, and kept its crews smiling too – a lot. This pair worked the winding main roads of Sussex from the small traffic base at Bexhill, where they were photographed late one afternoon. (PC)

While two livery variations deserve to slip under the wire.

A rare livery scheme was used by Cleveland Constabulary on this 1988/9 Vauxhall Nova and others in which white space between the three elements is used to create a unique compound stripe, wider than the sum of its constituents and very stylish – almost Brigade of Guards.

Commercial designers will have created Thames Valley's door and bonnet graphic and there are no complaints about their work – indeed, it deserves approval. It escaped selection earlier, as did the Omega II, which had its fans and certainly looked the part. (PC)

Ominously, as the previous photograph was being taken at Bicester traffic base, in the workshops behind me the last TVP Omegas were being dressed in the pleasing livery seen and the first TVP Omegas were being disfigured by hideous blue-and-yellow camouflage.

Truly the Golden Age

Sun-coloured at least, the livery on this 1970/71 Mk I Capri, belonging to Lancashire naturally, was near-perfect, according to research twenty years later. The best-known purchaser of Capris was Greater Manchester, which used sizeable batches of all three marks. Another devotee of sports cars, Sussex Constabulary, had a few.

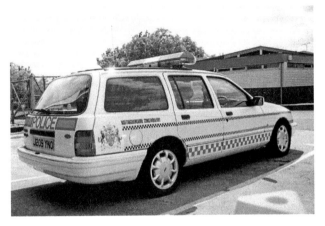

Already flagged as the finest coat of arms to appear on a British police car, Nottinghamshire's grant was happily similar to that of Nottingham City Police, whose cars had carried it since the 1930s. The restrained force titling style was long shared with distant Wiltshire. (PC)

Another livery coming close to ten out of ten was a Gwent combination. It was sad that this short-lived scheme didn't go fleet wide instead of some of the oddities that did, before Battenburg arrived. (PC)

The Golden Age saw some outstandingly attractive vehicles. Not to be left out is the reincarnation of the S-Type Jaguar, which usefully showcases West Yorkshire's almost Kent-style force titling. The typeface choice could have been more appropriate, but who's looking at that with a Jag to enjoy, however briefly. (JOC)

1995, Sussex. A chance encounter with an ultra-cool Cavalier III on the A259 near Winchelsea. (PC)

1995, North Yorkshire, Elvington Airfield. An Astra III in attendance at a VE Anniversary Day Fly In. (PC)

And Then Came a Long, Long Winter

The Golden Age of police vehicle livery was brought to an end because of official obsession with standardisation. For bureaucrats and administrators, it's a convenient and profitable obsession, providing work to do when there might not be enough and goals that may be achievable, whereas more useful ones may not be. To introduce standards requires research, committees, consultation, reports, more research, proposals, more consultation, drafting, implementation and compliance regulation; in short, work, and lots of it. Work requires people. Having more staff confers status – classic empire-building.

In the 1930s the Home Office tried hard to standardise police uniforms and iron out the interesting differences. The move largely failed, mainly because of local pride, assisted by the continuing independence of chief constables. In the 1990s attention turned to police vehicle livery. Very real operational and security advantages come from having different forces' vehicles positively identifiable. Conversely, to eliminate visible differences actually introduces unnecessary risks. Those and the cultural advantages of individual schemes were ignored in blind pursuit of a false ideal.

To bolster the cause, science was invoked. Boffins would determine the safest livery. This meant that any force refusing to adopt it would be seen as not caring for the welfare of its workforce and the public. In fact, the work had already been done by the Transport Research Laboratory, which had found that the paramount factor was that the complete outline of a car or motorcycle had to be clear for instant assessment of its position or the direction it was moving. This meant that, day or night, all the extremities needed to be in the same bright tone. According to these findings, Lancashire's orange cars of the 70s had been near-perfect and several of the 90s schemes were close to ideal.

The Home Office Police Scientific Development Branch, however, had different ideas. No doubt heavily influenced by reflective-material manufacturers keen to sell more of their expensive wares, these scientists came up with a diametrically opposed solution: Battenburg, which features large blocks of contrasting colours. Fellow scientists had used these before. In the First World War, ships had been painted with just such blocks for the purpose of disguising their shape and confusing attackers as to their direction of travel – they are actually camouflage, exactly the opposite of what was needed. Indeed they are eye-catching, but they are also eye-confusing. It can be appreciated by half-closing the eyes and looking at a vehicle or a photograph. A vehicle dressed in blocks ceases to have a recognisable shape. Most of the other pictures in this book will retain theirs. This was phoney science.

By 2012 most forces had succumbed to acceptance of the flawed national livery. London's Met had done so for traffic units but not across the board because of the extra cost of treating the huge fleet. Astonishingly the matter was decided by a public poll on social media – Londoners were asked to decide which they preferred. This begged the question as to why the rest of the country had been coerced into accepting the expensive blue-and-yellow blocks on the grounds that having them was necessary to ensure officer safety. If this were true, how could the decision in London be left to the aesthetic preference of the few people bothered to register an online vote – a vote that vested interests could presumably quite easily rig? The commitment to spend hundreds of thousands of pounds on an ongoing basis was, we are told, taken on the slim majority of seventy votes in a total response of just 800.

This Gwent Omega was one of the evaluation cars and had the full trial scheme. Note the red elements, which were a small attempt to restore the outline of the car, inevitably disguised by the blocks. Those red elements, arguably the most important, were deleted when the livery went live, presumably to reduce the costs of application to something slightly less astronomic. (PC)

But Nothing is Permanent – Fortunately

Battenburg in any form, but especially in the dreary, watered-down version that has been adopted, falls very far short of being the ultimate safe livery that its proponents would have us believe. All-orange or all-yellow police vehicles, as would be recommended by the TRL, are probably not acceptable aesthetically, although police motorcycles, where reinforcing a complete outline is many times more critical, have in many cases moved towards mainly yellow livery. For cars, white will probably remain the most effective base. White outlines can be enhanced with white reflective tape. Other than a minority of sidestripe designs, where they are so large that they interfere with the vehicle's outline, bold schemes can be good at gaining the attention of the eye without the drawback of confusing it, by emphasising the car's axis in relation to the viewer. Sidestripes could continue to reflect force identity, while large POLICE titling, especially across the lower panels of two doors, is the ideal way to project the generic message.

Battenburg is the 'King's New Clothes' and should be phased out. Good sense and good taste should return. If history is any guide, there's just a chance they might.

The Warwickshire livery was exceptionally effective by day or night. It left no doubts, and yet it did not dazzle or confuse. You knew you were looking at a car and not a signboard. You knew which way it was facing. It was distinctive and it was dignified. It did not demean the Royal Crown of the badge it carried. It was capable of any necessary enhancement without losing any of those attributes, and it did not pour unconscionable amounts of taxpayers' money into the coffers of mutinational material suppliers. (PC)

Recommended Further Reading

Bobbitt, Malcolm, *Police Cars* (Stroud: Sutton Publishing, 2001).

Dunne, David, *Armoured and Heavy Vehicles of the RUC 1922–2001* (Hersham: Ian Allan Publishing, 2007).

Green, Andrea, *M. G. S on Patrol* (Magna Press, 1999, New Softback Edn, 2011).

Hall, P. W., *The Police Range Rover Handbook* (Telford: British Bus Publishing, 1998).

Rivers, K., *History of the Traffic Department of the Metropolitan Police 1919–1974* (Andover: Phillimore & Co., 1974, New Edn, 2011).

Walker, Nick, *Those Were the Days ... British Police Cars* (Dorchester: Veloce Publishing, 2001).

Historic Transport Prints available from: PM Photography, PO Box 157, Camberley, GU15 9GJ.

Contacts

PVEC – The Police Vehicle Enthusiasts' Club
Information and Membership: Matt Holmes mattholmes600@btinternet.com
Archivist: Paddy Carpenter paddy.carpenter@gmx.com